The Camera
Never Lies

The Camera Never Lies

A BOOK OF EXTRAORDINARY AND BIZARRE PHOTOGRAPHS

Foreword by
CYRIL FLETCHER

Webb & Bower
EXETER, ENGLAND

First published in Great Britain 1982 by
Webb & Bower (Publishers) Limited
9 Colleton Crescent, Exeter, Devon EX2 4BY

Designed by Vic Giolitto

Translated from the French by Keith Cameron

British Library Cataloguing in Publication Data

The Camera never lies.
I. Photography
I. Title
779   TR145
ISBN 0-906671-43-4

Typeset in Great Britain by Busby's Typesetting and Design,
Exeter, Devon

Printed and bound in Great Britain by Hazell, Watson and Viney Limited,
Aylesbury, Buckinghamshire

FOREWORD
Cyril Fletcher

'Who is an authority on Oddities?' said Webb. 'There are Lewis Carroll, Edward Lear, Beachcomber and perhaps Cyril Fletcher,' said Bower. 'That last one is not in the same immortal bracket as the other three,' replied Webb. 'No,' said Bower. 'He's alive and I do not suppose he ever will be. But the point is he is getattable.' So that's why I'm doing this foreword. What they did not know is that comedians very rarely see other people's jokes. But I did here.

And I'm sure you will. The photographs are not all funny—the bizarre is mixed with the improbable. Here is the quintessence of quaint; the shock of the unlikely and the unfamiliar. The whole book is like a series of pages from recollected nightmares. Have we not all in dreams had back wheels race away from our cars at 60mph? 'Mr Raymond Mays noticed the back wheel coming off his car.' Glorious word that 'noticed'. And Mr Monty Bank's car is pure nightmare. The acrobat cyclist is cheating; surely his bicycle should be on fire. And does he not finish the trick by diving 20 feet head first into a pannikin of stewed rhubarb?

And what about Lucia, and the Living Statue of Liberty, and the skyscrapers, and the refrigerated fire, and those dogs trained to lie in the small of the back of a knife grinder? Suppose one of these trainers became unemployed. Can you see the supercilious sneer on the face of the clerk at the Job Centre when the chap says in answer to his query as to previous employment, 'I trained dogs to lie down in the smalls of the backs of reclining knife grinders.'

The lady on page 43 in the pre-Emmanuel gown (should she be blowing her nose on it?) appeals to me. Here is an idea for Women's Lib: take your babe to the office in your hat. I can visualize Esther Rantzen arriving at the *That's Life* studio with her latest offspring similarly and suitably ensconced.

As you turn each page you are surprised, amused, shocked, enchanted, intrigued, and find yourself beginning to laugh. Then you read the accompanying remarks and the tears dim the pages. Here surely is a best-seller. As surreal a best-seller as Surreal Fletcher could recommend.

Look at the last page, lingeringly with me. This proves the book to be after all a series of photographed nightmares. You think you are on a train, but you are on a boat. That often happens to me in a dream, only I find I am stark naked as well.

Don't Move

September 1907

Imagine how difficult it was to get these crocodiles to pose. For two days the photographer had to use all his skill and patience to take this group of four. By attaching lumps of meat to long strings on bamboo canes he managed to get them to come exactly to the spot he wanted.

The Double Jump of Death

June 1904

The inhabitants of Marseille were invited to watch a unique spectacle, the 'Double Jump of Death'. Inspired by the 'human arrow' which earned the acclamation of crowds in Paris, it consisted of leaping, on a bicycle, over an open space after pedalling down a slope. The attempt was not successful and the cyclist fell and was seriously hurt, suggesting that the stunt had been aptly named.

A House on the move

November 1906

Forced to leave his farm, a determined eighty-five year-old Basque farmer did not want to abandon the timber house in which he had lived for years, so why not, he thought, transport it with him to a new site. Thanks to an ingenious carpenter, the house was mounted on wheels, two pairs of oxen were harnessed to it, and it then began its journey towards a more hospitable environment.

A Mammoth Camera

May 1901

At the turn of the century Mr George R. Lawrence of Chicago built what he claimed to be the biggest camera in the world. A photographer, specializing in taking shots of high-speed trains, Mr Lawrence had found existing cameras too small to take anything but partial shots of each train. And so he constructed an apparatus as big as a hotel room. The camera weighed over 1400 pounds and the plates measured over 8 feet by 5 feet. It needed a team of fifteen men to load and unload it on to its special truck. Armed with a feather duster a man had to climb inside in order to clean it. The photographs produced were of extremely fine definition and precision.

The Child and the Mask

January 1916

War brought its problems to the little children of Rheims in France. Close to the front line, the town was constantly bombarded with gas and explosive shells. School went on as usual in the underground cellars, and the children were equipped with goggles and anti-gas pads which they carried with their lunch and books to school. As an added precaution they put their goggles on as soon as they left the house. Practice makes perfect. The older children helped the younger ones, and managed to put on their masks in thirty seconds.

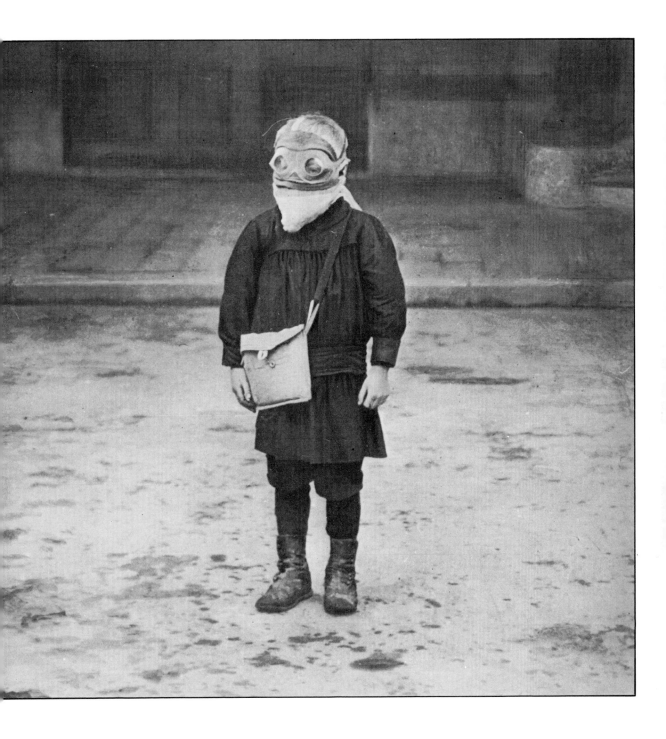

15

A Living Sculpture

July 1909

At the sea's edge a man is about to be sucked down by quicksand; the top part of his body is still seen protruding from the muddy wastes; vainly he tries to cling to the moving surface; his convulsed face raised to the sky, the frenzied look of terror in his eyes, his mouth open as he gasps for breath and utters useless cries for help—a traumatic picture of despair as a man prepares to die.

Taking as his inspiration Victor Hugo's famous phrase: 'To sink in quicksand is when a tomb becomes a tide and rises from the earth towards a living creature', the famous actor-sculptor, M. Capellani wanted to 'live' the part before commemorating it in marble. In the vast open spaces of the bay of Mont St Michel, he allowed himself to sink into the quicksands while the scene was recorded on film. The experiment almost ended in tragedy when the principal actor, the cameramen and the camera started to disappear into the mud. Fortunately, they were all rescued in the nick of time.

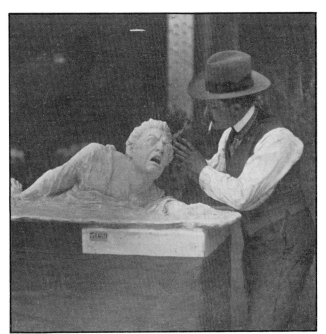

The Weighing of the Maharajah

March 1929

'Worth his weight in gold', a well-known saying which has been interpreted almost literally in India. The Maharajah of Alwar in East Rajputana had just celebrated his jubilee by distributing to the poor the equivalent of his weight in ringing, jingling rupees. A great deal of suffering was relieved by this considerable sum of money. So, if the Maharajah is worth his weight in silver, morally, he is surely worth his weight in gold?

A Visitation to the Nobel Prize Winners by the Goddess of Light

December 1930

Sinclair Lewis and the other winners of the Nobel Prizes were astounded on the morning of December 13 when a charming girl, dressed all in white, wearing on her flowing blonde tresses a crown of greenery with seven burning candles, brought them their breakfast. It was their first encounter with Lucia.

Every year, a queen, Lucia, is elected for one day from amongst the inhabitants of Stockholm. She is fêted and paraded at night through the gaily decorated streets of the capital. The evening closes with a supper dance—a necklace is offered to Lucia, well-known artistes recite poems in her praise, musicians compose waltzes in her honour, champagne corks pop, cheers break out and it all ends in a blaze of glory—next morning Lucia returns to her typewriter!

A Living Statue of Liberty

October 1918

A symbol in human form! Amazing but true, and requiring very careful stage managing. Over 18,000 soldiers assembled on the parade ground of Fort Dodge in the Des Moines Valley. Thousands of yards of white ribbon were fixed to the ground to form the basic shape and the participants took up their positions. The outlines of the fingers, the hair, the torch and the tunic were highlighted by rows of soldiers dressed in white—some with, some without a hat. The remarkable picture was taken by cameras mounted on a high platform. The laws of perspective had to be respected so that, out of a total length of 1230 feet, the body from shoulder to base measured but 150 feet and, somewhat incredibly, almost 14,000 of the total complement were grouped in the flame of the torch.

Not Afraid of Heights

August 1912

Seven hundred and fifty feet up on the Woolworth Building in New York. The workers have got used to it and don't appear scared or to suffer from vertigo. People, 'baby' skyscrapers and the streets below look minuscule in the background.

A Fire under the Ice

March 1908

The Headquarters of the Equitable Insurance Company in Broadway, New York, on the verge of being gutted by fire. It would have been an all too common disaster except that the weather was literally freezing cold, being several degrees below zero. When the firemen started their thirty-two pumps, they were covered immediately in a thick layer of ice; the great quantities of water directed at the building froze virtually on contact, in spite of the blazing inferno. This bizarre struggle between two elements would be hard to believe but for the camera's record.

'Hot' Dogs

December 1928

'All electric' may be the general cry but there still exist other forms of heat. Take these 'hot' dogs used by knife-grinders at Thiers in the Massif Central. The grinders have a unique method of working; they lie face downwards on a plank suspended over the rotating stone and rinse the blades in a mountain stream which has been diverted to run through the workshop. In winter they are exposed to the cold and to help prevent rheumatism they have, for as long as anyone can remember, trained their dogs to lie in the small of their backs to provide them with a source of gentle heat all through the day. The animals are biding their time for, as soon as the warmer weather arrives, they are transformed from heating into hunting dogs.

The Dog Man

February 1904

Theodore Petrof was known to circus-goers throughout the world as Jo-Jo. Alleged originally to have been found running in a wild state in the Russian forest of Kostroma, Jo-Jo was taken into captivity with another monster who appeared to act as a father to him. The dog-child was sent to school where he learnt Russian but never lost his original accent or his strongly guttural tones. At the age of eight he was 'discovered' by an impresario and started his life of being exhibited as a freak.

The front of his head was shaped like that of a dog and covered with fawn-coloured hair which gave him that spaniel look. And yet his hands and feet were exceptionally graceful. It is a pity the Russian Church did not allow an autopsy: science might have learnt a great deal.

The Long and the Short

March 1905

It is surprising whom you meet backstage in the London Hippodrome. Could any couple be more ill-assorted than Chiquita (2ft 4in) and her gigantic companion Machnof (9ft 4in)? To keep up his strength and his 27½ stone, Machnof has a daily menu which would make the heartiest eater turn pale—30 eggs, 7 pounds of meat, 5 pounds of vegetables, 5 pounds of bread and 3 litres each of beer and tea.

The Child Giants

July 1907

When Wilfrid Westwood and his pretty sister Ruby from New Zealand popped in to see their paternal grandfather in Wednesbury, near Birmingham, they caused quite a stir.

The 'little girl' is 5ft 2½in tall and weighs 17½ stone, yet she is not thirteen. Wilfrid, aged ten, is even taller and heavier; in fact, he weighs more than his normal-sized parents together.

Apart from their size, the children play normally with their comparatively dwarf contemporaries; and coming from the North Island, they speak both Maori and English perfectly.

Bounteous Nature

November 1933

Nature generally does things well but sometimes she does make mistakes, providing too much here, not enough there. The Arab in the photograph has a set of thirteen fingers, enough to turn any aspiring pianist green with envy. But his generous supply of toes could make some women wince at the thought of having to fit them into a tight-fitting shoe.

A Strange Case of Motherhood

July 1910

When two Siamese twins, Rosa and Josepha Blazek, were being exhibited in Vienna one of them gave birth to a little boy. A gallant Austrian carpenter admitted to being the child's father. The birth provoked a certain amount of comment. The baby boy was, however, perfectly normal.

39

Collaboration from an Unexpected Artiste!

November 1924

Auguste is the protégé and star of film director Alfred Machin. Auguste was a born actor and he could create irresistibly comic effects—he will shower maternal affection on a little child or pretend to be angry, jealous or desperate; he can appear sad or to be in ecstasy; he passes effortlessly from clownishness to serious drama, from hilarious comedy to poignant tragedy.

In the photograph he is 'starring' with actor of stage and screen, Maurice de Feraudy, who is playing alongside a chimp for the first time. When interviewed, M. de Feraudy claimed that he knew no one 'more intelligent, more impish, more subtle nor more affectionate'.

A Cradle in the Air

November 1919

We are familiar with pictures of African women who carry their children around on their backs. But the women of Peru place their little offspring, comfortably installed in wide baskets, on their heads, maintaining the balance by walking along with a slight lilt. They are naturally supple and gain experience by carrying water in the same way from a very early age. What happens when the child leaves the cradle? The cradle is not abandoned, the women continuing to wear it as a hat.

An Odd Snapshot

August 1924

An unusual car race over Caerphilly Hill near Cardiff in Wales. After trying to take a corner at sixty miles per hour, Mr Raymond Mays noticed his back wheel coming off his car. He was able to control the steering and stop without an accident. He was lucky, as was the alert photographer.

Mountaineering in a Car

June 1929

Skiers on the slopes around Chamonix were surprised on one occasion to see Monty Banks, the English comedian, skiing in front of the cameras. They were even more surprised when, a few days later, they discovered a car perched 3000 feet up the valley. Transported by cable car, the car was supposed to have attached itself accidentally to a sleigh and to have been dragged to the edge of a cliff with a drop of several hundred feet. There it wobbled and swayed as Monty Banks and his stooges gave a display of hair-raising antics.

The only subterfuge for this outstandingly dangerous piece of filming was to attach the vehicle very firmly to the rock—no wonder the onlookers felt somewhat anxious.

47

The Car Leap

February 1921

It is not usual to see a car jump over any obstacle it may encounter. Such a facility would have been particularly useful during the war. Coincidentally, a French mechanical engineer did invent a car with what he calls a 'propellent suspension'.

The photograph shows a car taking off, like an aeroplane, at a speed of 22 miles per hour. After taking a 3-foot-inclined slope, it rises about 4ft 6in into the air and (as can be seen in the second photograph) lands some 15 to 20 feet away, the rear wheels perfectly level with the front ones.

49

A Horse versus Horsepower

August 1927

An unexpected contest on the La Capelle racetrack. The horse led most of the way, but on the last corner the car managed to take the lead and beat it by a few yards.

It was an amusing experiment but is it a useful one? What is at stake, the skill of the driver or the adaptation of the car? If it is the latter, then it could be of great interest to the car industry.

Between Saddle and Earth

November 1934

Three stages in the space that separates a jockey in his saddle from the turf. First, the rider shoots off into space like a missile; second, he appears to twist his body so as to soften the landing; third, he hits the ground. Notice how he was holding so firmly on to his mount's bridle that he ripped it off its head as he sped through the air. The camera can certainly reveal interesting facets of an everyday occurrence!

The Jockeys' Double

December 1908

A scoop for the alert photographer at Kempton Park when just after clearing a fence after the mile mark, two jockeys left their saddles at the same time, leaving their bewildered mounts still standing. Fortunately, they escaped with a few bruises.

A Spectacular Fall

August 1932

The place: the Olympic Games in 1932. The moment: the Hungarian competitor, Petnehazy, stumbled over a fence and his horse took a vertical nosedive. After remounting, the rider finished the competition and was reasonably placed. The lesson: even the most experienced should be careful.

On Horseback in Space

October 1929

Some like to make it tough! Some like to go down rather than up. The Marquis of Los Prujillos seems to be one of the latter. The drill captain at the Spanish School of Cavalry is seen here descending the almost sheer face of a 40-foot ridge. To accomplish such an exploit, horse and rider must have a heart and legs of iron.

The Acrobat Cyclist

September 1906

Crowds in Buffalo have been treated to a new, breathtaking stunt. Schreyer, the Daredevil, designed the apparatus himself. It consists of two inclined planes built on scaffolding and reaching a height of over 100 feet. 80 feet away from the 200-foot-long track is a small pool, 16 feet by 10 feet and 5 feet deep.

Schreyer descends the first slope on his bicycle, pedalling furiously. As he begins to ascend the launching pad a warning pistol shot rings out, by which time he is already about to 'take off'. He lets go of his bicycle, glides for a second in mid-air and then dives straight into the middle of the pool. It is all over in ten seconds

The most difficult part of the trick is to judge the exact moment at which to push away the bicycle.

A High Dive into Shallow Water

August 1908

Holidaymakers were amazed to witness a fantastic dive by Peyrusson at Joinville-le-Pont, near Paris. From a 100-foot-high platform, the diver plunged into space, first horizontally and then adopting a normal diving position about 30 feet from the surface of a 9-foot-deep pool. His record-breaking exploit could have cost him his life: the impact as he hit the water was so great that half his clothing was dragged off and his left arm remained paralysed for four minutes, but he lived to tell the tale.

Jumping in the New Year

February 1930

Is this picture upside down? No! Professional acrobats practising in the open air? Wrong again! It is merely the members of the San Francisco Olympic Club celebrating the New Year in their own way. The members of the largest club in California have got into the habit, every January 1st, of going for a swim in the warm waters of the Pacific. After their dip they give a healthy display of sporting activities and gymnastics. What better way to get rid of a hangover?

Aquatic Acrobatics

April 1930

Surf riding has long been popular. People jumping about in the foam, as they hang on to the guiding rope, often look like the charioteers of old.

Yet, in Florida, the blasé exponents of the sport have tried to make it more difficult and more interesting. One of them has attached a wing with strong supports to an aquaplane; drawn along at great speed by a motorboat, the aircraft takes off and glides through the air at a low altitude like a kite. Perfect balance is not easy to maintain and a fall could be disastrous, if not for the flying man, at least for his machine.

How to go over the Niagara Falls

July 1928

Jean Lussier going over the Niagara Falls in the presence of 150,000 spectators. He did it inside a rubber balloon. It had two air compartments and was big enough for him to be able to sit inside. The sphere was launched from the side of the river, and went into midstream where it bobbed about on the turbulent waters. It disappeared into the foam and for a moment it was thought that it had become wedged between the rocks; then all of a sudden, it appeared at the base of the falls where it was whisked away by a waiting boat. Its occupant was virtually unconscious and the attendant doctors thought he might have broken his back. But he quickly recovered.

The Amphibo-cycle

January 1909

The problem of how to plough through water on a bicycle has been solved by a young inhabitant of Lyon. He has reached a speed of 5½ miles per hour on his amphibo-cycle which, as the name suggests, is a vehicle equally at home on water as on land. Basically it is a bicycle with floats, and has a propeller activated through an ingenious system of pinions by the back wheel. It has also a reverse gear and the steering is made possible by a rudder placed against the front wheel fork.

Relatively lightweight (110 pounds), it can be changed, at will, from a bicycle to a boat.

The Podocaphe

May 1907

When canoes were all the rage, sportsmen used a 'podocaphe' made from two completely flat canoes joined together. Mr Raymond of Montelimar perfected this form of transport and used it to hunt waterfowl or to fish. From the way he slipped it on as though it were a pair of shoes, this seemed to be a comfortable and useful invention.

The Milkman on his Round

December 1930

The Seine, on December 2, 1930, reached almost 20 feet, and as soon as the danger level of 17½ feet was attained, sand bags and pumps were put into use. Several villages in the suburbs were flooded but life goes on and the milkman does his daily round.

The Amphibian Car

April 1931

Before undertaking a trip half way around the world, Captain Geoffrey Malins tested a very simple device to allow his three cars to cross stretches of water.

Each car was suspended by a system of balloons, some round, some oblong, attached to rods like extended bumpers. There was also a central supporting rod beneath the middle of the vehicle. The car was thus easily transformed into a sort of raft. The problem of propulsion through the water was solved by attaching metal blades to the car wheel which then acted like the paddles of the old boats or watermills.

The main advantage of this invention was its convenience. All the material could be packed up into a small space and could be assembled and taken apart by the occupants of the car.

A Piercing Encounter

August 1932

At the speed races in Chicago, a speedboat driven by a contestant from Milwaukee went careering, like an arrow, at a speed of 45 miles per hour into a 36-foot-long motor boat. The pilot was thrown into the sea, whence he emerged safe and sound. By a miraculous stroke of luck, not one of the passengers in the perforated vessel was hurt by the unexpected torpedo.

Prisoner of the Sea

April 1931

No! This is not Noah's Ark, but a Chinese junk which, at the height of an exceptional October tide, anchored off the port of Amoy during the night. Imagine the surprise of the sailors when, in the light of day, they realized they were perched on a rock some thirty feet above the level of the sea. We can but hope that they managed to refloat their ship at the next high tide.

Good for Scrap

September 1910

The SS *Princess May* appears to be stuck hard and fast. Her keel is firmly wedged between two rocks and although the right propeller is in pieces, the hull is intact.

It has been suggested that it might be possible to free her with explosives but the experts are doubtful about the chances of success.

Balloons in Collision

July 1909

Crowds at the balloon race organized in the Parc du Cinquantenaire in Brussels in July 1909, were witnesses of an extraordinary accident.

Jumping the gun, the balloon, *Cosmos,* collided with a statue on top of one of the columns. This made an enormous rent in it and the half-deflated balloon collapsed on top of another, the *Busley;* as it did so its anchor made a gash in it, releasing the gas which started to envelop the four passengers in the *Cosmos.* Two of them had the presence of mind to jump out on to the *Busley* and slid, with great gymnastic agility, to the ground. The remaining two were virtually overcome by the fumes and when the basket eventually reached the earth they were in a bad state. Fortunately, they soon recovered.

A Strange Trip through the Air

June 1932

Goodyear-Zeppelin are forging ahead with the development of their second cruiser airship, modelled on the *Akron*. The *Akron*, an airship built by Goodyear-Zeppelin, was at one time assigned to the Navy where it was used, albeit with certain mishaps, on active service. While trying, unsuccessfully, to stop over at Fort Kearney in California an unfortunate incident occurred. Three sailors in the operation team did not let go of the stowing cables in time. As the airship regained height, two of them lost their grip and fell to their death; the third, Bob Cowart, managed to wrap the end of the 300-foot cable around him and thus get hauled aboard the air-cruiser. He can be seen clinging, with justifiable determination, to the end of the hawser.

The First Flight of the 'Aviette'

July 1921

Competing for the 10,000 francs Peugeot Prize, Gabriel Poulain has, after a lot of experiment, succeeded in raising himself from the ground by auto-propulsion on an 'aviette' or little bicycle equipped with wings. With an estimated take-off speed of 25 miles per hour on his 37½-pound machine he reached a height of 38½ feet and 40½ feet. The wings apparently encountered considerable resistance and the aviator-cyclist had to make tremendous efforts.

A Floating Plane

July 1909

This photograph was taken from the torpedo boat *Harpon,* while the lifeboats were being launched to go to the rescue of the pilot and his machine. Hubert Latham was not perturbed; for twenty minutes he waited patiently and smoked a cigarette. His only discomfort when his plane touched down at sea—wet feet. To avoid contact with the water all he had to do was sit up a little higher on the back of his seat. For once the Straits of Dover have been merciful to their victim.

An Aeroplane 'midst a Game of Bowls

August 1911

This charming French lady pilot has just had an unfortunate, if amusing, accident.

During an air display at St Etienne, her engine failed suddenly at an altitude of about 300 feet. She was forced to land on the bowling pitch of a nearby café, damaging a young acacia tree but not herself or the plane. She seems to have brought more pleasure than panic to the smiling spectators.

93

A 554-hour Flight

July 1930

The Americans have long been recognized as specialists in records for long distance flying with in-flight refuelling. In 1929, Dale Jackson and Forest O'Brien set up a record in St Louis of 420 hours 17 minutes; now, in Chicago, the Hunter brothers John and Kenneth have raised the record to 554 hours with the *City of Chicago*. For twenty-three days and two hours, they circled over the airport, being refuelled in flight by their brothers Walter and Albert and eating food prepared by their sister Irene.

The interest of the exploit resides in the fact that a single-engine air-cooled production model flew 45,000 miles in a variety of atmospheric conditions. The apparent repair in mid-flight which is the subject of the photograph seems to have been effected more for the curiosity of the public than out of necessity. In fact, the flight was terminated because of a break in the fuel feed.

Vercingétorix Travels by Bus

December 1901

Bartholdi's statue of the Avernian hero has just begun its long journey from the Jaboeuf foundry in Paris to Clermont-Ferrand; its first stop will be the Grand Palais in the Champs Elysées where it will go on exhibition.

When it was discovered that it was not possible to send it by rail, the problem of transporting this huge work of art (20 feet high and 15½ feet long) was solved by constructing a special vehicle. The De Dion-Bouton 'bus' has a 35 horsepower engine and it was calculated that it would take 5 to 6 days to get to Clermont-Ferrand at a speed of 6–7 miles per hour.

Hanging by a Thread

November 1913

For some time now, transporter bridges have been used to link up two sides of a valley; along the cables suspended from the pylons travel electric cars bearing all sorts of goods, sometimes even passengers. But how daring can you get? The photograph shows a locomotive swinging over the Grand River Canyon in New Mexico. It weighs 20 tons and is supported by trolleys 300 feet above the water and hanging on wires suspended from pylons 1300 feet apart. Yet it only took a flick of an electric switch to send the enormous load to the opposite bank. Somehow man's ingenuity is enhanced by the majestic grandeur of the setting.

A Meal for 26,000

November 1904

26,000 guests at a gargantuan celebration organized by the Mutualité Insurance Company. A few details will serve to convey the magnitude of the occasion. 1500 waiters walked around 13 miles of tablecloths serving 1½ tons of hors-d'oeuvre, 820 feet of sausages, 5000 poultry, 200 pigs, 42,000 fruits, 1½ tons of *petits fours,* ½ ton of dried fruit, 1 ton of sugar, and 4 miles of bread rolls. There were 19,000 gallons of liquid refreshments and the evening finished in smoke with almost 8000 feet of cigars. No mention was made, in the statistics, of indigestion tablets.

7000 Cattle at Longchamp Racecourse

September 1914

After an initial shortage during the early days of mobilization, food supplies returned to normal, the price of meat remained stable and that of other foodstuffs comparatively low. It seemed that the chances of Paris being besieged were low because of the state of the army and the size of the town. However, if it should happen, then famine was not to be feared. Various racetracks were requisitioned right at the beginning of mobilization and were converted into cattle enclosures. Eventually 7000 cattle were at Longchamp, and throughout the Paris area piles of fodder and herds of animals brought a touch of the peaceful countryside to the capital.

The Stork with the Wooden Leg

June 1907

A somewhat unusual stork. When her leg was crushed she was given a splint but complications occurred and it was necessary to amputate the leg at the knee. Her owner then fitted her out with a wooden leg and she hopped around as agilely and as happily as before. She even has a spare 'peg-leg' just in case!

The Hand Game

November 1931

It is claimed that the parrot is one of the few representatives of the feathered race to possess understanding. It is the only one, in any case, which has not completely lost, since the fabulous times of yore, the use of speech and it may be this fact which leads us to believe that it may have glimmers of thought... at least our picture would tend to support this belief for the biped is playing 'Hot cockles' with what is a traditional quadruped enemy. The kitten even appears to eye her adversary's beak with some apprehension. They may be playing but old fears die hard.

A Duel between Water Monsters

February 1927

What went wrong? Normally this type of crocodile, found in Arnhem Land, Northern Australia, does not attack either man or its own kind. But here the two adversaries were locked in a fight until death. The victor managed to grip his opponent's jaw with a tremendous vice-like hold and to force him down beneath the surface of the water where he eventually drowned.

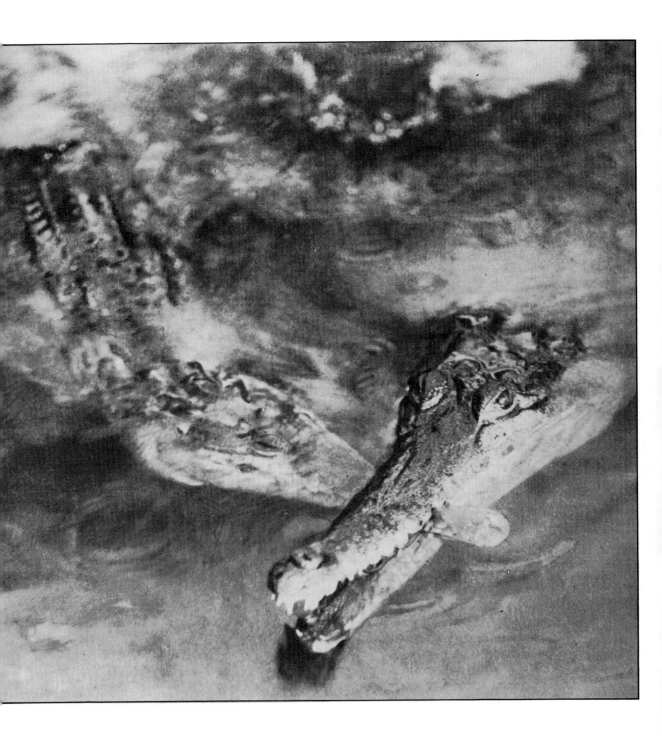

The Human Net

September 1933

Americans are very fond of making geometric shapes out of humans and then photographing them— flower petals, the Stars and Stripes, etc. On this occasion, girls in a swimming pool have formed a large meshed fishing net. They are vertical in the water with their arms spread out; and when photographed from a distance it makes a perfect optical illusion. Is there any need to add that this spectacular effect was produced for a Hollywood film?

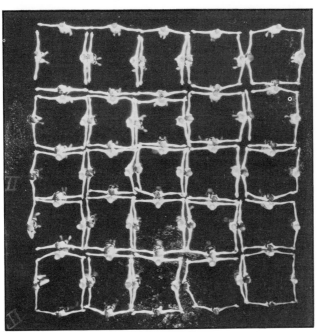

Nature Gives a Wink

May 1935

Nature plays strange tricks at times. These human masks are in a bed of pansies in the Persian Garden of the Samarkand Hotel, Santa Barbara, California. The 'masks' are merely flowers with wide-open petals whose delicate designs provide caricatures of the human face. Do you recognize anyone?

The End of a Star

January 1927

The death of Auguste (see page 41) caused genuine mourning at this Nice studio and here he is to be seen on his deathbed, surrounded by flowers. With him are his former companions at work and at play—another chimpanzee, a faithful dog, and Cloclo, Alfred Machin's son, who first played alongside Auguste in a film when he was only eighteen months old. The assembled friends are paying homage to one who possessed almost human intelligence and feelings...

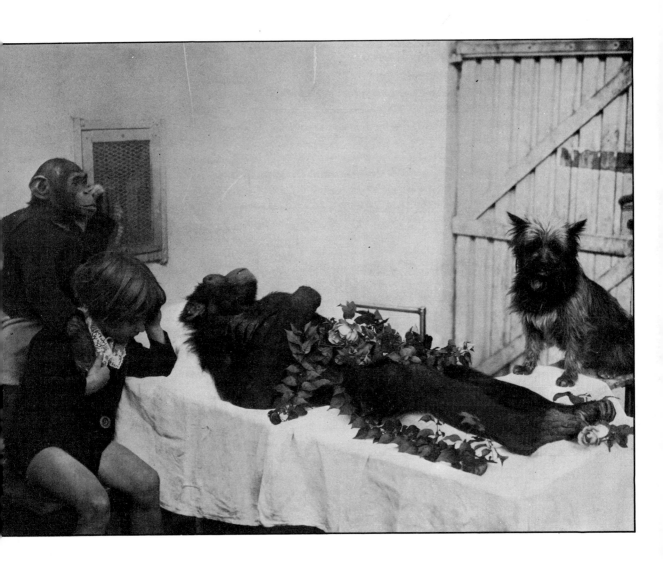

117 and Still Squawking

October 1913

Parrots do live a long time but the one shown in the photograph must be the oldest of the species. At the time of the photograph Cocky Bennett was at least 117 years old, and a celebrity in Australia. According to the Brisbane weekly, *The Queenslander,* Cocky was born in 1796, near Sydney, and was taken from his nest way up in the lofty branches of a eucalyptus tree by a local farmer. Five generations later, he still belonged to the same family.

    Cocky did not age well; his feathers dropped out, his skin became wrinkled and his upper beak grew so long that he could only eat mashed foods. And yet, even at such an advanced age, he was still chirpy and greeted the guests with a 'Welcome, gentlemen!' as he hopped around on the top of his cage, shaking his featherless stumps.

The Boat Train

January 1926

You think you are on a train and it turns out to be a boat! The passengers' faces reveal their anxiety as they follow the train's progress through flooded countryside. They are probably afraid of getting into even deeper water.